Ana Castillo

I Ask the Impossible

Ana Castillo is the author of the novels *Peel My Love Like an Onion, So Far from God, The Mixquiahuala Letters,* and *Sapogonia.* She has written a story collection, *Loverboys;* the critical study *Massacre of the Dreamers;* the poetry collection *My Father Was a Toltec and Selected Poems;* and the children's book *My Daughter, My Son, the Eagle, the Dove.* She is the editor of the anthology *Goddess of the Americas: Writings on the Virgin of Guadalupe,* available from Vintage Español *(La diosa de las Américas).* Castillo has been the recipient of numerous awards, including the American Book Award, a Carl Sandburg Award, a Mountains and Plains Booksellers Award, and two fellowships from the National Endowment for the Arts. She lives in Chicago with her son, Marcel. Find out more about Castillo at her homepage: www.anacastillo.com.

Also by Ana Castillo

FICTION

Peel My Love Like an Onion

The Mixquiahuala Letters

Sapogonia

So Far from God

Loverboys

POETRY

Otro Canto

The Invitation

Women Are Not Roses

My Father Was a Toltec

NONFICTION

Massacre of the Dreamers:
Essays on Xicanisma

I Ask the Impossible

I Ask
the Impossible

POEMS

Ana Castillo

ANCHOR BOOKS
A Division of Random House, Inc.
New York

FIRST ANCHOR BOOKS EDITION, MARCH 2001

The following poems have appeared in these publications:

"I Ask the Impossible" and "Peel My Love Like an Onion" in the *Berkeley Poetry Review* (Issue 26, 1991–1992). "A Federico García Lorca más a algunos otros" in *The Berkeley Review* (1991–1992). "Since the Creation of My Son and My First Book," in *Frontiers: A Journal of Women's Studies* (Volume 13, Number 2). "You Are Real as Earth y más" in *Puerta del Sol* (New Mexico State University, Volume 27, Number 1) and in *New Mexico Poetry Renaissance* (Crane Books, 1994). "El Chicle" in *The Massachusetts Review* (Volume 36, Number 4) and as part of the Poetry Society of America's Poetry in Motion series. "Mi volador," "On the Meaning of Things," and "Death Is Only What It Is" appeared in *Poesída* (OLLANTAY Press, 1995). "Nani Worries About Her Father's Happiness in the Afterlife" and "Seduced by Nastassia Kinski" appeared in *After Aztlan* (David R. Godine, 1992). "Burra, Yo" titled here as "Burra, Me" and "Waterbird Medicine" appeared in *Shards of Light/Astillas de Luz* (Tía Chucha Press, 1998). "For My Child Who Became a Man in His Thirteenth Year" appeared in *Power Lines: A Decade of Poetry from Chicago's Guild Complex* (Tía Chucha Press, 1999).

The Library of Congress Cataloging in Publication Data
Castillo, Ana.
   I ask the impossible : poems / Ana Castillo.—1st Anchor Books ed.
     p. cm.
   ISBN 0-385-72073-4 (alk. paper)
    1. Mexican American women—Poetry. I. Title.

PS3553.A8135 I15 2001
811'.54—dc21

                       00-061790

www.anchorbooks.com

Designed by Cassandra J. Pappas

Printed in the United States of America
10 9 8 7 6 5 4 3 2 1

Acknowledgments

I would like to thank Madame B., wizard of Russian blood who was reincarnated as one the hardest-working literary agents alive. See you next time around. Also, *mis gracias sinceras van a* Robin Desser, my editor, and to her staff for their passionate support, which has made putting these poems together such a pleasurable experience. I am honored and grateful to the distinguished poet Rosario Ferré for the translations of my Spanish poems. I would be remiss not to mention my friend Elsa Saeta, who holds down the fort and always has my gratitude from near and far. *Con todo corazón*, I thank Nilda for our ranchito hideaway. Always at my side, my son, Marcel Ramón, has been growing up, as it shows in some of these poems. I am also indebted to those who have passed on and who are also remembered in my verses. As well, there are those who lift my heart by their example who are very much alive and appear in these poems prominently or between the lines. To them I send a ray of light, love and peace with my gratitude. Not only people but places, too, are thanked for their inspiration. These poems are for all of them, *con mucho* love.

—ANA CASTILLO
Summer 2000

¿Quién dice que todo está perdido?
Yo vengo con mi corazón.

—Una canción

Contents

Introduction	xv
I Ask the Impossible	3
El Chicle	4
No Dogs or Mexicans Allowed	5
Waterbird Medicine	6
Mi volador	8
You Are Real as Earth y más	9
A Nahua Woman's Love	11
Anna Mae Aquash	12
Nothing But This at the End	14
The Desert as Antidote: Verano, 1997	16
A Small Scorpion	19
I Heard the Cries of Two Hundred Children	20

"Never Again a Mexico Without Us"—
Comandante Ramona 22

1999 26

Burra, Yo 29

Burra, Me 31

La Burra confunde la amistad con un cuerazo 33

La Burra Mistakes Friendship with a Lashing 34

La Amiga regresa a educar a la burra 35

The Friend Comes Back to Teach the Burra 36

I Did Not Think She Was Beautiful—Then 37

Coatlicue's Legacy 39

"Like the people of Guatemala, I want to be free of
these memories . . ."—Sister Dianna Ortíz 41

¿De quién es la paz? 47

Whose Peace Is It? 49

I Saw Perú 51

Dear Pope: Open Letter from the Americas 53

Los Angeles: A Report 55

Recipes for a Welfare Mother 56

Women Don't Riot 58

Cabrona con corazón/Goat Woman
with a Heart 61

Since the Creation of My Son
and My First Book 63

For Marcel Ramón from His Mother at Sea 66

La Wild Woman 67

What Is Not Found in Paintings or Books 69

Tatehuarí 70

Tatehuarí 72

I Decide Not to Fall in Love 74

Y¿dónde se encuentra Dios? 75

Where Can We Find God? 76

On the Meaning of Things 77

Hummingbird Heart 78

Nani Worries About Her Father's Happiness
in the Afterlife 79

Día de muertos 81

How Does It Feel to Be Cruel to a Woman? 82

For My Child Who Became a Man
in His Thirteenth Year 83

A Little Prayer for the Trees 85

For Alberto and Selena 86

Death Is Only What It Is 87

Peel My Love Like an Onion 88

Los Tocayos 89

For Elsa 90

I Am Not Egyptian 92

All I Have for Her Is a Poem 93

María's Clock Is Alive 94

Seduced by Nastassia Kinski 95

One Thousand Nights 97

When Women Part 99

For a Toltec Queen 100

She Was Brave to Leave You 101

While I Was Gone a War Began 103

A Federico García Lorca más a algunos otros 106

For James Baldwin, with Love (November 8, 1989)   109

Poeta en Santa Fe   110

Chi-Town Born and Bred, Twentieth-Century
    Girl Propelled with Flare into the Third
    Millennium   111

Canto para las brujas of Good Deeds and Desires   119

Introduction

These are meditations, odes, stiletto stammers, and *disparates*. They are my shot of aged tequila at the end of the day and hints of a *bruja*'s *hechizos* in the black night under a new moon. They are the musings of a big-city gal and the prayers of a solitary woman who can feel equally at home in the desert or rancho.

The poems in this collection were written between the years 1989 and 2000. During this time my son grew up into a tall young man with long fingers for playing the cello. We relocated numerous times around the country while I was teaching. I worked on a variety of book projects and in between I kept up with my poems: I filed them. I reworked them from one year to the next. Once in a while I'd let one go out into the world for publication. I destroyed several—with the same impulse I had of writing them to begin with—just because the mood had struck me to do so. Poetry, like my painting, was my indulgence. It was also, like my painting, often my companion and my refuge.

I did not study literature in college. Politics and the workings of the world were my turf. Over twenty years ago, I decided to write mostly in English because many Latinos raised in the United States were not schooled in Spanish and were uncomfortable with reading it. At that time I saw them as my primary readers. But Spanish belongs as much to my daily life as the frijoles and tortillas that can always be found in my kitchen. I once heard that the language you count with is your true language or that the language you argue in is the one you really command. Some say it is the language you speak when making love. (Although I have doubts about this last litmus language test since the Latin Lover is such a stereotype I suspect some use Spanish for that reason!) I have retained the language of my ancestors sometimes to the surprise of people who do not know that you can be born in any city or country and keep your mother's tongue, as was my case. I am very honored that the distinguished writer Rosario Ferré has translated the Spanish poems I've included here.

When I started taking writing in verse seriously nearly three decades ago, I wrote as a witness to my generation. I felt as if I were the red-tailed hawk that I have spotted some mornings on a ranchito. It is visible, despite its ruddy camouflage, sitting on the highest limb of a dead tree. I know it is watching me, too, with a keener eye than my own because that is its nature, to perch and watch. When it spots its prey, it swoops down. That was me—the young poet swooping down with widespread wings. My poems turned to stories and sometimes stories demanded entire novels.

Here you have the seeds and sloughed-off snakeskins of some new stories.

Today, for many, one view of the world seems too binding

where freedom of choice seems to be everyone's last hope and first right. What does that say of that sense of commitment, loyalty to a specific community that so marked cultures in prior centuries? People experiment with religions that have nothing to do with ancestral heritage. We relocate to new places for the sake of a job, not to plant roots. When a better job comes along, we pick up stakes and move again. Not only people but also nations as we have come to recognize them have changed their entire identity. Countries like Yugoslavia, Tibet, and the Soviet Union, for example, have been disassembled or absorbed. China is being repackaged for new markets. And on and on. . . .

Speaking for myself on any given day I do know this: nearly three decades ago as an art student I moved to the urgent jotting of verses as witness. I hope that my poems still serve as testimony to the times.

I imagine I will always write my idiosyncratic, pertaining to no-school-that-I-know-of brand of poetry. It gives me enormous pleasure to share it with you.

—ANA CASTILLO
Summer 2000

I Ask the Impossible

.

I Ask the Impossible

I ask the impossible: love me forever.
Love me when all desire is gone.
Love me with the single-mindedness of a monk.
When the world in its entirety,
and all that you hold sacred, advise you
against it: love me still more.
When rage fills you and has no name: love me.
When each step from your door to your job tires you—
love me; and from job to home again.

Love me when you're bored—
when every woman you see is more beautiful than the last,
or more pathetic, love me as you always have:
not as admirer or judge, but with
the compassion you save for yourself
in your solitude.

Love me as you relish your loneliness,
the anticipation of your death,
mysteries of the flesh, as it tears and mends.
Love me as your most treasured childhood memory—
and if there is none to recall—
imagine one, place me there with you.
Love me withered as you loved me new.

Love me as if *I* were forever—
and I will make the impossible
a simple act,
by loving you, loving you as I do.

El Chicle

Mi'jo and I were laughing
ha, ha, ha—
when the gum he chewed
fell out of his mouth
and into my hair
which, after I clipped it,
flew in the air,
on the back
of a dragonfly
that dipped in the creek
and was snapped
fast by a turtle
that reached high
and swam deep.
Mi'jo wondered
what happened to that gum,
worried that it stuck
to the back of my seat
and Mami will be mad
when she can't get it out.
Meanwhile, the turtle in the pond
that ate the dragonfly
that carried the hair
with the gum
swam south on Saturday
and hasn't been seen
once since.

—*1995, New Orleans*

No Dogs or Mexicans Allowed

We were on our way to Laredo from Chicago
when the bus stopped at a diner in Texas somewhere.
Mami and I got off quietly,
the way we did things then, unobtrusive,
the way we always have
done things or left them
undone. Inside, as the rest ate, we waited
and waited
while no one took our order.
The driver called out:
"Everyone on board!"
and it was time to go.

Mami took my hand and hurried me along
so as not to be left behind. We
did not eat that afternoon.

That was a long time ago.
But my memory is probably better than a dog's.

—1996, *Chicago*

5

Waterbird Medicine

Peyote is in my blood
my brother told me, the one
who made me a gift
of a silver and sapphire waterbird at dawn.

For immeasurable time, fire—
sapphire, gold, and amber snakes
turned to ash, swept into the shape
of a waterbird—was life.
There, I saw us:
the way we are together,
fire,
life,
a waterbird of holy ash.

Staff, gourd, and drum were passed,
and each singer cried more than sang
his prayers.
But mine were not sung.
I drank my prayers,
tasted them beneath my tongue,
an acrid paste of mesquite.

Waterbird—sweeter than the wildberries and
dried beef passed round when light broke at last,
fire,
water,

Sangre de Cristo morning air—
gliding over Blue Lake,
carry my sole prayer: I am silver and sapphire:
        a woman on fire—
        and more worthy than stone.
        Bring my lover to me soon.
        Ho!

        —1990, *Albuquerque, New Mexico*

Mi volador*

Death wears the mask of a young man,
color of burnt maize—

He takes my prayers to the sky—
with a rope about the waist, flies
down to Earth again.

Ehecatl, I call him.
We laugh like macaws,

I am a cloud of rain,
full with him.

And he—without me—
is only crazy wind.

—1991, Albuquerque, New Mexico

*Papantla Flyer. In an ancient sport of the Totonac, five young men dressed
as macaws climb a pole. One plays the flute at the top while the other four,
with one end of a rope tied to a platform at the top, the other around their
waists, unreel their way to the ground in a sacred ceremony.

You Are Real as Earth y más

I

A green chile ristra
you are, 'manito—
hung upside down,
on a rustic porch.
Rock, you are,
coyote, roadrunner,
scorpion stung
still running strong. Sometimes,
you are a red ristra
into whom I take burning bites
and always yearn for one
more
bite.
You are real as earth y más.
You are air and sky. While I—
who have traveled so far to reach you,
remain the blood of fertility,
fear of your mortality,
pungent waters in which,
you believe, you will surely
die a godless death.

II

And when you are neither sky,
nor warm rain,
nor dust or a pebble in my shoe,
you are the smoke
of an old curandera's cigar

trailing throughout my rooms.
You are the Warrior Monkey
in a Chinese Buddhist tale; you are
copper and gold filigree—
Tlaquepaque glass blown
into the vague shape of a man,
a jaguar, a gnat. I
look for signs to see if it is really you.
Tonantzin appears as Guadalupe
on a burnt tortilla.
Coffee grounds, wax, an egg dropped
into a clear jar of water.
I look for signs everywhere.

III
I have lit farolitos to guide
you back to my door.
Turned upside down by desire,
it seems your feet
are on a groundless path. Beware the Trickster.
The road in either direction
is neither longer nor shorter,
nor more narrow nor wider
than the fear that closes your heart.
Gray ash sediment in my entrails,
this path of ours is Sacred Ground.

—1990, *Santa Barbara, California*

A Nahua* Woman's Love

A Nahua woman loves tough like corn husk left in the sun.
She wears a throbbing necklace of hearts and hands.

When you want her most—her laughter hurts
like hail against your head.

A Nahua woman loves more soothing than desert rain.
She is turbid as chocolate and yerba buena wise.

She sees with a third eye.
You may call her yours and sometimes, she doesn't mind.

The Nahua woman is Tepeyac—a miracle flourishing
out of rock in midwinter—

and you will want to say—Mother, although she is not.
After death, when you become cinder and pulp,

and your soul—a snail toiling along huihuitl bark,
you will still be her lover. Don't be alarmed.

Don't try to get away. There is no hole where she
does not wait on the other side.

—1992, *Albuquerque, New Mexico*

*Of the people who speak Nahua, living today in modern central Mexico.

Anna Mae Aquash*

(For Ronnie Burk)

When it snows, I think of you,
frozen angel, no hands.
Micmac witness,
whose eyes sealed shut
by the cold forever,
were closed
with malice.
More than that—
more than my heart
that trembled
when I read of your death,
a generation ago.
My frozen angel,
on your land persists
a civil war.
Your land, as barren
as a grandmother,
still, was your land.
Your witness became rumor
with your assassination.

*Anna Mae Aquash, a Micmac Indian rights activist. On February 24, 1976, Aquash's body was found on the Pine Ridge Reservation in South Dakota; she had been shot in the back of the head. The circumstances of her death remain a mystery. Her hands were cut off and sent to FBI headquarters in Washington, D.C., for possible identification. The FBI accused the American Indian Movement of killing her because it was believed she was working for the FBI, while AIM accused the FBI of murdering her in retaliation for the deaths of two FBI agents shot near Oglala, South Dakota.

How do you kill an Indian woman
when you carry a gun legally,
are a government agent,
and are on her land?
You track her down
one night when
no one is watching,
like an animal for trapping.
Aim for a main artery,
put three, four bullets in her, grab
the black, stringy Indian hair,
take an ax,
whack off the right, then the left
hand. Teach them all a lesson.
Bury her face,
pumpkin-round Indian face,
in the snow.
Let the winds blow a drift over her body,
her underfed Indian body,
the bloody, perforated coat, the sanguine stumps
of her arms,
dot-dot the white snow,
drench the white snow.
My frozen angel,
with wings as wide as memory,
I think of you always,
in the white-white of snow.

—1997, *Chicago*

Nothing But This at the End

My eyes were spellbound
on a well of dark blood
gushing from a black bruised arm
gushing like oil
in a dialysis center.
A woman in house slippers
and a face like an ancient ritual mask.
She made me afraid,
which turned on its head
made me brave.
But it wasn't me bleeding.
Black and brown flesh
and blood all around.
We have the worst diets
in the nation.

"Don't ever get fat," Mami told me
from her chair
where she was attached to a machine
with a false kidney.
All it is is a plastic cylinder.
There's no smell of freshly cut grass
in that room,
no trio serenading from one
patient to the next,
no baptisms or weddings to plan,
no more menudo on Sundays after Mass.

Nothing but the silence of that woman's
gushing,
Mami's hand touching mine,
pushing me gently. "Go home now."
Nothing but this at the end.

—1997, *Chicago*

The Desert as Antidote: Verano, 1997

I

Cabuches picked from the big-headed biznaga plant
or served with vinaigrette on a plate
taste divine!
Thimble size
bright yellow
tiniest pineapple crown
a claret burst of bliss inside.
Tonanztin, our Great Mother, took delight the day
she kissed the cactus
and made it bear fruit.

One day Our Mother made prickly pears:
green fat thumbs
that cling to the nopal.
She dyed some red for fun.
In the desert I sucked on one
along the way.
This poem is my thanks.

II

One thing I won't eat
is the *chiniquil:*
a half-inch worm with one
black eye
or behind.
I can't tell which end is which.
It's snatched from the maguey

a delicacy in Mixquiahuala
dead or alive.
But not for me.

  III
Sometimes animals eat animals
to survive the sierra,
except chickens. They eat anything.
Don't stop at a ranch without a
white flag.
The horses are hungry.
Ranchers sic dogs on strangers
who only want to stop
for a drink.

Lightning strikes in all directions.
The rain god Tlaloc's daggers
split the horizon.
It's easy to get lost
with so much going on
in the sky.
A good thing to know
is how to whistle.
Someone will find you.

Huitzilopochtli glared down
at my hat. The sun god is full of wrath
at midday.
We took murky water from a ravine,
disinfected it with lime,

but by then,
half-mad with thirst,
we didn't care about germs.

—1997, Chicago

A Small Scorpion

A small scorpion ran inside my blanket
while I slept beneath
a veil of meteorites,
made love to me
all night
with its tiny
penis
its tiny tiny tongue
I did not feel
a thing
even when it
stung.
I did not die
and neither did
the scorpion.
We just went on
with our lives
after that.

—1997, *Chicago*

I Heard the Cries of Two Hundred Children

I heard the cries of two hundred children
bleating in the desert.
They were not two hundred but two thousand,
not one at all, not
so much as a lost shepherd
with a skinny herd of goats
but only the wind pretending
to be the ocean's roar.

I heard more
of the cry of children's ghosts
the ones who sleep on cathedral steps,
and who swerve through traffic,
little clowns and fire-eaters,
wash windshields
with contaminated water and shine shoes
with hepatitis spit, pick pockets
in the metro and pull your sleeve
on the street
while behind a dark window of the Palacio Nacional
the president looks out
concerned about the national deficit,
a highway built by narcotrafficking kings,
and the latest accusation of election fraud.

I heard the children's cries in the desert
but it was a storm

like storms can be in the desert
majestic and terrible,
lightning swords pierced
the horizon.
Three swords went through my heart, and
came out on the other side.
You think you are alone in the desert
but you are not; so many eyes watching you.
Every thorn,
cactus worm, scorpion hides.
The withering snake, the wide-winged crow
in the sky, coyotes call to each other
in the dark.
The sky too is watching you.
Coyolxiauqui Warrior Queen
does battle each night,
her four hundred children stand guard.
Are they who call you,
and not Mexico's young,
not the ghost of your mother at eleven
who scrubbed floors for a plate of food?
Is that you? I call, and I think someone answers.
I think it is her, my dead mother
marching across the Tropic of Cancer,
marching with four hundred sky children,
feasting on the wind.

—1997, *Chicago*

"Never Again a Mexico Without Us"
—Comandante Ramona*

DÍA DE LA RAZA, 1996, MEXICO CITY

The poorest of the poor,
her kidneys rotted,
heart tied in cotton,
tongue in tzotzil
Comandante Ramona: ¡presente!

One hundred thousand waited to hear her,
one hundred thousand with
or without medical services
provided them
and their children;
one hundred thousand
who can read
unlike Ramona,
take buses freely unlike Ramona,
go to school,
join a union,
operate machinery,
a computer, car, telephone
unlike la Comandante Ramona—
who has come to say:
"Give something to my people,
not to me
who can do one thing that

*On October 12, 1996, Comandante Ramona, a leader of the Zapatista uprising that took place in Chiapas two years before, presided over the Second National Indigenous Congress held in the zócalo of Mexico City. At least one hundred thousand attended her address.

no one will object to now,
that no one will prevent,
who can only die,
am dying
as I speak.

"Take care of the rest,
the ones who carry wares to the market
as we have since time began,
but are being stopped
with our baskets of chayote,
chile, and bolts of cloth,
at the crossroads
by the military.
They do not let us pass.
We are raped instead,
left by the road,
warned not to come back,
not to trade,
not to eat,
not to live.
The roads too, ancient and paved,
destroyed now.

"I beg you
save their water
deliberately defiled
with animal feces,
poisoned,
to teach us a fatal lesson.

"Take care of the children,
and the old ones
who cannot care for themselves.
And to the men who can—
allow them each a small plot of land,
And the women—leave alone.
That is all we want, all that we ask.

"If not us, let our descendants
live like human beings.

"I came to say these few words," she said.
"'So small and yet so important'
they called me. So sick to come
so far from her home.

"It is a new century,
not one year of despair,
not ten, but hundreds.
Still, nothing is done.
Whites preach that God
helps those who help themselves,
as the whites have helped themselves
to land,
and that which is found beneath
deep in the earth's entrails, and
that which grows above it.
They helped themselves to the blood and toil
of the people.
They let us die.

And when we would not all die,
they sought ways to kill us.

"I've broken silence,
picked up arms,
laid them down
for a little justice,
a little justice.

"What more can we do?"
La Comandante asked,
before she went silent again.

—1996, *Chicago*

1999

By the end of the twentieth century
a few months short of its end
I found myself
trembling, trembling
all the time.
I trembled as if with fever
like when I had
walking pneumonia
one summer
and didn't know what
was wrong,
just that I couldn't
stop
shaking.

By the end of the twentieth century
I looked around,
was nearly blinded by the
persistent whiteness
all around,
the weight of whiteness
all around
white and powerful
like African diamonds
and I shook, as I said,
all the time.

I didn't want to talk
about the shaking.

I was taught
not to complain.
I didn't want to alarm
anyone,
those who might
care, who might
worry.

If I watched the TV
or put on the radio
or turned on the
computer and
went on-line
before long I
was not only shaking
but feeling a little sick, too.

I couldn't
for the life of me
figure it out.
All I know is that I
felt so very tired
so very tired,
and then I started
trembling all the time.

I looked around and no one
was very happy,
not even the young,
not even those who had
comforts,

especially not those with
political status.
If I squinted,
if I squinted like this,
I swear, everyone looked
like they were shaking, too,
if only
just a little bit.

They looked very tired,
even the young,
even babies
in their carriages
looked tired
and old.

I looked up, squinting,
and the bald sun, too,
of course, was trembling.
Why not? Its days were
numbered by all accounts.

When the moon was full
and let herself be seen
I watched her. She was
weeping outright.
And I
kept on trembling
inexplicably and without
consolation.

—1999, *Chicago*

Burra, Yo

Burra, yo.
Burra fea
burra flaca,
y floja.
Burra que sirve solo
para cargar
la mierda de este mundo.

Burra, yo.

Burra—
Conténtate que tienes de comer,
que casi no te golpean,
y cuando sufres es por tu bien.
Así llegarás al cielo más pronto.

Burra, tú.

¿Cuándo has visto una burra
con collar de perlas,
anillos de rubís y diamantes?
¡Qué cosa más ridícula!

¡Ay, burra, burra!

Lo tuyo es un saco de harpillera
zapatos de fierro,

y latigazos en abundo.
Acabo no lo sientes, cuero de burra.

Cabeza de burra.

Y cuando duermes, sólo sueñas
los sueños de burras.
Las burras son piedras con patas
sin imaginación.

Acéptalo de una vez y quizá
Dios te perdonará
por haber nacido tan

Burra, burra.

Burra, Me

Burra, me.
Ugly burra.
Thin as a bone
and lazy.
Burra that's got
no business except
carrying the shit
of this world.

    Burra, me.

Burra—
Be grateful you've got something
to eat,
that they hardly ever
beat you;
when you suffer it's for your own
good.
That way you'll reach heaven
faster.

    Burra, you.

When have you seen a burra
with a pearl necklace,
ruby and diamond rings?
How ridiculous!

    Ay, burra, burra!

You're the hemp sack type,
iron shoes,
And thrashings galore.
Don't tell me you don't know it, you burra pelt.

Burra head.

And when you dream, you only dream
Burra dreams.
Burras are boulders with feet . . .
and no imagination.

You might as well
accept it and maybe God
will pardon you for having
been born so

Burra, burra.

—Translated by Rosario Ferré

La Burra confunde la amistad con un cuerazo

Y un día alguien llegó y quiso darle
un cariñito a la burra—

Le pasó la mano
tratando de acariciarla.
Le habló con una voz de dulce.

Pero—la burra por ser sólo una burra—
no reconoció la ternura,
y le dio una patada bien dada
a la pobre amiga que pensó
que las burras podían sentir.

La Burra Mistakes Friendship with a Lashing

And one day someone came and tried
to give the burra a cariñito—

She stroked her
and tried to caress her.
She spoke to the burra with a sweet voice.

But the burra—because she was a burra—
didn't recognize the tenderness
and gave a good kick
to the poor friend who thought
that burras could feel at all.

—Translated by Rosario Ferré

La Amiga regresa a educar a la burra

Al siguiente día (y a pesar de la patada
no merecida)
regresó la nueva amiga de la burra,
la única en el pueblo.

Traía con ella tres zanahorias y una cajita de truffles.
—Tú sabes, burrita—le dijo, con una voz
más fina que la harina blanca,
—No tenías por qué rechazarme—
Miraba a la burra comer,
esperando una respuesta.
Pero la burra simplemente pegó un rebuzno.
Así se comunican las burras.

—1990, *Santa Barbara, California*

The Friend Comes Back to Teach the Burra

The next day (in spite of the free
kick she got)
the burra's new friend
came back,
the only one she had in town.

She brought with her three carrots and a small box of truffles.
—You know, burrita—she said, with a voice
as finely spun as white flour,
—You didn't have to reject me—
She watched the burra
as she ate, waiting for an answer
but the burra, being a burra,
simply brayed.
That's how burras speak.

—Translated by Rosario Ferré

I Did Not Think She Was Beautiful—Then

(Para mi mamá, en memoria)

I did not think that she was beautiful—
then. Arms too fat,
top full lip shapeless red. Heavy
lidded eyes, my inheritance.
But that woman
of my long ago
in the photograph next
to the eternally handsome dad
with drunken gaze
is luscious to me, now.
No wonder he loved her so.
Although he did not
tell her,
show it,
even when she asked.

In the mirror I am a little more like her
with each year that's past.
At the beautiful woman's funeral
women comfort me.
Big-armed women. Women with painted lips.
Sirens who weep with me,
who keep men at bay,
who love whom they may love
when and if they please.

She taught me these things and more.
Strength is a woman, a seed in a box
buried in the ground in a thunderstorm,
buried deep in my heart.

—1997, *Chicago*

Coatlicue's* Legacy

(Para las discípulas)

I am Coatlicue's daughter
and reigning priestess
but sometimes I forget.
Sometimes someone puts a hand up
that falls hard against my face
and I forget
that within me
is the word and
tomorrow he'd be dead.
No doctor would have helped.
His mortal mother, beside herself.

Sometimes I forget
all I need to do is say it
think it
breathe it
dream it
and life is at the hem of my stone skirt,
a drifting feather
four hundred warriors strong.
It waits for me to spread my legs
wide as a wild-eyed spider
PUSH
      heaven to hell

*Coatlicue: Principal Aztec deity, the formidable goddess of fertility and destruction

PUSH
     God's soul through me
PUSH
     the sun down to China
PUSH
      Earth's axis round
      like a spinning top.

And life is in my hands,
suckling at my breast,
thrives on the rhythm of my beating heart,
warmth of my throbbing belly.
Bite that cord or not
bury the placenta or not
spit out the skeletons of bad boys
or shit them out—
who did not learn to honor
Woman,
but fear Her just the same.

Sometimes I forget
when I've been robbed and raped
to numbness
that mine is a terrible wrath.
And that blood begins
and stops between my legs.

                               —1997, *Chicago*

Like the people of Guatemala,
   I want to be free of these memories . . .

—Sister Dianna Ortíz

Every morning we rise
out of our warm beds,
in Minnesota, Chicago,
Los Angeles, perhaps,
wrapped in the security of
our flag, secure in the dream
that we are and always will be safe.
We have simply to rise and work hard,
if only the world took our example.

Once a year, we take out our passports
and plan vacations,
to visit friends and relations south.
We do not think that by chance,
a case of mistaken identity, let's say,
a wish for peace expressed too loudly,
disdain for a government
uttered without discretion,
we might end like Sister Dianna Ortíz,
whose crime was to be an American citizen,
a schoolteacher—
who can say—
in a country the size of a pearl,
a poor beyond poor country,
populated by a dispensable race,
undergoing civil war.

But she did not commit a crime.
No government ever accused her of any.
The official report is
that nothing happened.
Instead, it is claimed, she is insane,
a woman given to hysterics:
A crazed lesbian who put one hundred
and eleven cigarette marks on her own back,
or a sadistic lover in the convent
burned her out of passion.
It makes more sense
than a nun being abducted from her
courtyard without explanation one afternoon
when the sun fell on the red-shingled roof just so,
and the children had gone home,
but some had stayed for the bread
the madrecitas bake,
and others always stay
because they have nowhere to go,
more sense than being raped
by a pack of dogs in uniform
like a stray bitch in heat,
burned one hundred and eleven times
with cigarette butts,
thrown in a pit,
yes a pit,
like a lamb
is thrown in a pit
for a Sunday picnic.
But the lamb,

once slaughtered,
a merciful cut to the throat, is
placed with greater care
than was Sister Dianna Ortíz,
half-naked and burned, and
yes, by then,
crazed.

She fell on other bodies,
some alive, some beheaded,
rats eating the rest.
This is what is known as the nightmare from which
a person does not, will not, could not
awake,
and what followed next
has no name.

Rise, at peace with yourself,
if you will, tomorrow.
Be content with your president,
your local officials,
the small and big things that they do.
Complain during elections
about what they do not.
But don't think of Sister Dianna Ortíz
or the soldier who put a small machete
in her hand. Yes, it is time
to die, thought the nun, let me die.
And she prayed an Our Father
or rather, addressed the same Supreme Maker

that you or I or any American citizen
might address at the hour of our death.
The soldier's hands around hers
that held the small machete that
was not used on her own body,
swung it forward instead and she slashed
another woman, also in the pit,
saw the woman's blood
spurt out like the blood of a pig,
felt the woman's blood,
still warm with heartbeat,
spray her face,
tasted it on her teeth
as she heard the woman's screams
mix with her own.
Who was shouting loudest?
Sister Dianna Ortíz did
not know.
She did not know.

Now, years later, she sits in vigil
on government steps,
your government and mine,
in Washington, D.C.,
and wants to know
precisely
who screamed loudest.
She wants to know
why human beings in Guatemala
are slaughtered

like pigs on Saturday,
why civilians are made sacrificial lambs,
and why a gringo saved her at last
like a knight but who was not
a knight. He was the chief of those
she says burned her,
violated her from body to soul,
although they did not take her soul.

Those—soulless themselves—
who have mutilated women, hungry children,
unarmed civilians, la raza indígena,
the illiterate,
unskilled,
bewildered and besieged
for four decades
or have given the orders to do so
or provided the means
did not take her soul.

Like the people of Guatemala, I want
to be free of these memories.
I do not want to lose my soul,
traded so cheaply here,
when we rise out of our snug beds
and do not question who the gringo was
who drove Sister Dianna Ortíz to safety,
who told her he, too, cared
for the people of Guatemala,
and wanted to save them from communism,

at any cost,
and who, those who seized her—
burned her one hundred and eleven times,
threw her in a pit with rats and cadavers,
made her kill,
then pulled her back out and laughed
as they took turns with her again,
and again—
called the gringo Chief,
and asked him to join in on the fun.
He was an American.

Let us shout louder than her memory,
louder than the unheard cries
of 200,000 disappeared,
buried alive in pits,
thrown alive from planes,
butchered and bayoneted
defenseless and blindfolded
in the name of democracy.

It is real, the nightmare,
and without end.
How can we sleep?
How can we sleep?

—1996, *Chicago*

¿De quién es la paz?

¿De quién es la paz?
Sino de un puñado de hombres
que firman tratos de negocios. El
que ganará más
y él que se tiene que
conformar con menos.

La paz
para tí y para mí,
los que antes fuimos diez
y ahora somos dos,
es un silencio púrpura,
por la madrugada,
el salir a la finca,
a la maquila, a la montaña
a convertir en polvo
ese día en noche,
manos callosos, pies
pulidos como piedras.

La paz para tí,
es una tumba,
enterrada viva.
El batallón de Neptuno,
te queda por sobrevivir.

Para un pueblo caído
la paz
es una nube gris en el cielo.

Y yo, escribo estas cuantas
palabras
en la tierra
antes de que se me olvide
que la tristeza no lo es todo.

—1991, *Albuquerque, New Mexico*

Whose Peace Is It?

Whose peace is it?
If not of a handful of businessmen
who sign treaties. He who gains
the most and he who must
accept less.

Peace
for you and for me,
We who were once ten
and are now two,
is a purple silence,
at dawn,
as we leave the farm,
the sweatshop, the sierra
that turn to dust that day
from night,
hands full of knots, feet
as smooth as stones.

Peace for you
is a grave
buried alive.
Neptune's army
is still to be survived.

For a fallen people
peace is a gray cloud
in the sky.

And I write these few
words
into the earth
before I forget that sadness
isn't everything.

—*Translated by Rosario Ferré*

I Saw Perú

I saw Perú, a closed eyelid,
from Lima to Cuzco,
on a train ride, parched
as dried grass.
Skinny spotted cows,
sterile chickens,
dirty children ran, ran
to catch a piece of fruit
thrown by a tourist
from the train
going fast, past them forever.

Thousands of grubby potatoes at the market
and barefoot Incan descendants
with derbies and broad-rimmed bonnets—
I saw. Cobalt blue colors, sunflower yellow dyes
and bright spices,
wrapped in a bit of brown paper
for a small price.
Everyone toothless and shy.

I heard Bolivian tunes throughout
over the airwaves and live,
sung by the blind for a few *soles,*
sung for a hope.

And dust everywhere,
along the banisters in cathedrals and museums,

in the president's palace. The entire plumbing system
backed up to Chile, out to Colombia,
so that the very young
and very old pee in broad daylight.
Beaches of Lima strewn with glass and garbage.
Cabdrivers warn tourists—don't stay out too late.

Let them eat *choclo*! someone seems to have declared,
and a small piece of fried trout on special days.
They may have instant coffee but not ask for milk.
The starved cows in the field have none to give.
No one has much to give but a smile
with a "Please, *mamita linda,* won't you buy
a freshly made tamal? No meat, of course,
just cornmeal . . . c'mon, don't be mean."

—1998, *Chicago*

Dear Pope:
Open Letter from the Americas

Querido Papa: We are bound to you, the multitude of the
    Americas,
the barefoot and patricians, the imposing politicians,
like a rosary binds a matrimony, she, promising to obey,
he, to protect.

Papa, you do not protect when you send us to our death,
with a disease that seems a consequence of human desire.

Who protects adolescent girls in Honduras, thimble of a country,
who slave to support their families? They are forced to take
    contraceptives,
sterilized, driven to a cancerous end. When they die, Papa,
    young and anonymous,
do you condemn my little sisters?

Is there forgiveness for the adolescents in Juárez for prostitu-
    tion when toiling
in maquilas was not enough to feed their families, and they
    are found dead
in garbage dumps, cheap panties stuffed into their mouths?

How many candidates for beatification would you have if all
those girls said no, "I'd rather die, let my mother die,
my father, my baby starve?
I will not give up my virtue for the sake of beans and a pound
    of cornmeal.
I will stay faithful to my church no matter what."

And the nice lady of the house, the one such girls
in every country clean for, who does not even think
of these sins because she eats and sleeps as she pleases—
if she is raped in her bed one night, tied and sodomized
in petrifying darkness, fertilized with sperm while being
    strangled,
a knife at her throat—will you send her away if she does not
    carry out
a pregnancy?

Slaves who miscarried in the fields or in the mines,
were stoned to death on the steps of your church.
Papa, you are a historian, do you remember the Conquest
of the New World? Some scholars call it the Conquest
of women, because that is when women became a thing to
    own.
And Papa, one last inquiry about the mysteries of sex,
I ask, as a mother and sinner, you, who are eminent and wise,
unfettered by the profane, tell me this—
if I were a good wife, the mother of all the children God sent
    me,
devoted and clean of heart,
why would my passion for my beloved be an offense to God?
Animals mate solely to procreate, Papa, not human beings.
I know you are not a man of science, but if you can and if
    you will,
answer these few things.

                                                    —1998, *Chicago*

Los Angeles: A Report

Today, October 4, Mrs. Jones
went berserk.
She took her three-year-old daughter
into the bedroom, locked the door,
and with a kitchen knife
stabbed her to death.
Next, she took her four-year-old daughter
and killed her just the same.
Mrs. Jones had gone berserk, but despite this,
she could not go on.
So she forced her eight-year-old son
to take the same knife,
and do to her as she had done
to his sisters.
At first, he refused. But she insisted.
Finally, his six-year-old brother as witness,
he let the knife into her
again and again,
until she was dead.
The boy called the police and said
his mother was hurt.
No charges were pressed.

—1988, *Oakland, California*

Recipes for a Welfare Mother

Corn bread: flour, water, mix.
Bake three times a day.
Beans: pinto, red, black, or white.
Add water, soak overnight.
Make enough to last all week.
Grilled cheese sandwiches with government cheese product.
Skip grill if there is no bread.
Always use lard, white sugar,
have Coca-Cola and powdered donuts on hand.
They'll make your breasts hang,
send your posterior out to Canada,
your gut to the Mexican border if
cancer doesn't get you first,
your children and aging mother.
Mix: AIDS virus, hepatitis B, tuberculosis,
impurities as a result of a malfunctioning kidney
into your bloodstream,
dissipate slowly.
You can stay home or work for minimum wage,
your diet will stay the same.
Your life will be the same.
You will climb the same dirty stairs,
drink contaminated tap water,
sit in the same stained tub,
bathe with laundry soap.
Be hot in summer, freeze in winter
until your heart explodes

one night in your sleep,
like an illegal firecracker.
Merengue music playing so loud next door
no one will have heard it.

—1997, *Chicago*

Women Don't Riot

(For N.B.S.)

Women don't riot,
not in maquilas in Malaysia, Mexico, or Korea,
not in sweatshops in New York or El Paso.
They don't revolt
in kitchens, laundries, or nurseries.
Not by the hundreds or thousands, changing
sheets in hotels or in laundries
when scalded by hot water,
not in restaurants where they clean and clean
and clean their hands raw.

Women don't riot, not sober and earnest,
or high and strung out, not of any color,
any race, not the rich, poor,
or those in between. And mothers of all kinds
especially don't run rampant through the streets.

In college those who've thought it out
join hands in crucial times, carry signs,
are dragged away in protest.
We pass out petitions, organize a civilized vigil,
return to work the next day.

When women are sterilized, have more children
than they can feed,
don't speak the official language,
want things they see on TV,

would like to own a TV—
women who were molested as children
raped,
beaten,
harassed, which means
every last one sooner or later;
women who've defended themselves
and women who can't or don't know how
we don't—won't ever
rise up in arms.

We don't storm through cities,
take over the press, make a unified statement,
once and for all: A third-millennium call—
from this day on no more, not me, not my daughter,
not her daughter either.

Women don't form a battalion, march arm in arm
across continents bound
by the same tongue, same food or lack thereof,
same God, same abandonment,
same broken heart,
raising children on our own, have
so much endless misery in common
that must stop
not for one woman or every woman,
but for the sake of us all.

Quietly, instead, one and each takes the offense,
rejection, bureaucratic dismissal, disease

that should not have been, insult,
shove, blow to the head,
a knife at her throat.
She won't fight, she won't even scream—
taught as she's been
to be brought down as if by surprise.
She'll die like an ant beneath a passing heel.
Today it was her. Next time who.

—1998, *Chicago*

Cabrona con corazón
Goat Woman with a Heart

I come from a long line of goat women,
an entire migration
moving north since the beginning of time.
We're everywhere now—
although the public would prefer
not to see us—
With our unsettling glare,
dark and graying fur.

No one feels my horns right away,
is ever left to bleed,
trampled on without thought or mercy
but meets an end swift and clean.

Goat women are outspoken,
sometimes defensive,
picky,
always a little hungry,
and the most uneasy trait
of all: stubborn.
We climb obstinately,
slips don't defeat us,
are good in packs
but a goat woman
doesn't hesitate to trek alone
along the narrowest ledge.

I read in a magazine once
that we are never satisfied.
They say we don't cry,
demand too much.
Look out for those cabronas, it read.
They've got voter cards,
licenses of all kinds,
a goat woman bare-breasted on the cover.
Still, you couldn't see her heart.

We do have hearts,
the size of watermelons,
that don't fit in the chest cavity.
Some find its exposed arteries,
its thumping, annoying.
There are cabronas con corazones
and then there are cabronas.
Don't mistake me for the kind
without a heart.
But no mistake about it,
sí soy cabrona.

—1997, *Chicago*

Since the Creation of My Son
and My First Book

At 4:00 A.M. there was water. He—because I knew he was a
   he—
was nine weeks early. We, who planned our delivery at home,
went by ambulance to a hospital. They tested us, tried to drug
us. They took blood from us,
stuck tubes in every orifice, put us
in isolation and watched us for five days.

As always, we were alone.
(I spoke in plural like God in Genesis.)
On the fifth day for twelve hours we struggled to separate.
He was strangling on the umbilical cord. I vomited.
No anesthesia, just he and I trying to part.
I did not cry. Instead, I thought of the ocean and how much
I would like to see it again.
(A promise I made to myself if I got out of there alive.)

My tiny baby had no name.
He lived in a glass box with a tube through his nose
and down his throat for twenty-one days.
His mother received no flowers for her victory.
She left the hospital on her own feet the day after his birth.
Empty-handed but with swollen belly and painful breasts.

They don't take hospital pictures of premature babies.
What does it mean that all this went so unnoted?
My son and I. Our first separation.

For the reception of my first book, I stopped breast-feeding
and flew to Texas. Our second separation.

Now he is seven and with his father. They live
in another city, another state, across the country.
Taking turns is the modern way to live.
Mothers are indeed dispensable.

I am a poet who doesn't sit in cafes.
I don't like nightclubs.
I live alone.
I am almost always filled with my son,
who is abstract and mostly memory between visits.

I write all the time.

My father died one year ago. He is not abstract.
His absence also fills me.
I don't read much as of late.
There is a war going on. On another continent.
No doubt I will write about it,
Not many friends in this new town to distract me.
I have had PMS for three days.
If I drink myself into a stupor, who'll know?

In dreams, I chase a crazy rabbit into a hole
and find a wondrous world. One in which I am not in debt.
I once changed diapers and had no hot water.
I once wrote poems in a basement with no heat.
I once had a lot more enthusiasm.

I have almost always been
unemployed. Those who are curious about a poet's life:
There you have it.

—1990, Albuquerque, New Mexico

For Marcel Ramón
from His Mother at Sea

Sneaky, sneaky sea
snuck up on me
talking to the crab,
tiny fish, clear as gelatin.
The sea still furious
from last night's storm
it washed me to shore
on two feet!

The crabs that have eight
and manatees that have none
had no choice but to go back
into its monstrous arms,
got sucked into the very womb
and heart of such
a sneaky, sneaky sea.

—1997, *Chicago*

La Wild Woman

(Para Clarissa)

She had just read a book which impressed her very much,
so much la Wild Woman let her *chongo* down—
llorona-style—and left the third of her husbands and four chil-
    dren.
She went wailing through the night.

Wearing hand-stitched moccasins,
a skirt slit down the thigh, she picked up a Wild Man from the
    mesas.
He was really wild. He had wild hair, a silk shirt opened to the
    navel,
and best of all, was how he played fandango.
With his guitar in hand the wild couple went off
to a wedding fiesta.

That night la Wild Woman drank a lot of wine,
and danced like Rita Hayworth in a movie,
all alone and barefoot, shaking her hips.
Meanwhile el Wild Man tried to sneak off
with la Bride (who politely declined).

Dressed in antique lace
and with an apparent taste for the truly refined
la Bride had also caught la Wild Woman's eye,
who was now intoxicated by all that la Bride possessed,
which—la Wild Woman shrewdly assessed—
went *beyond* gifts of silver platters and candlesticks,
monogrammed linen and picture frames.

La Wild Woman twirled and twirled inebriated by the
purple chamisa in bloom along the cerros, roasting red chile
in August—
cactus that stays firm beneath winter ice and blossoms in
spring, drunk
on the bride who sat aloof and so sublime
with such black hair and painted red lips, she made her
dizzier still.

The mariachis played while the groom talked business in the
parlor,
and bowls of posole were passed around to the guests.
The waxing moon rose higher and higher
driving la Wild Woman to the cliff of her imaginings.
So . . . there was only one thing left to do.

La Wild Woman stole a horse from around the back
and with a swish and a grunt she took la Bride in tow.
All was chaos and uproar or maybe, in truth, no one noticed.

Wait—wait! called the bride as she reached for some cake
and a bottle of champagne and together they rode off
without a saddle.

—1994, *Albuquerque, New Mexico*

What Is Not Found in Paintings or Books

Perhaps I should not call love what
we have concocted, you and I
like a tea prescribed in an obscure shop on Grant Street.
A handful of small sticks, roots, dried flowers,
put in a ceramic pot to boil until it is thick as tar.
You hold your nose to drink the tar-tea
which nevertheless keeps you alive.

You have promised to forget me once again
and once again you seek me out,
just as quickly disappear.
If this love or rabbit trick
that you and I perform
through the years had eyes
they would be very large.
As it is ours alone it stays
insatiable and blind.
And for the idly curious: paintings
and books conceal more than they ever tell.

—1997, *Chicago*

Tatehuarí*

Tatehuarí
vino y me dijo—
¡Muchacha!
Si no era yo tan viejo
como los cerros,
la sierra
el mero peyote
yo mismito
te tomaba
como mía.

¡Muchacha!
Este hombre negro
como chocolate
tiernito
como el nopal guisado
te lo entrego.
En él estoy yo encarnado.

Ya que las nubes
no tienen carne
ya que el aire
no es de huesos
ya que te quiero

*Dios antiguo de los Huicholes.

como te quiero
y tú estás en el mundo.

Yo en el reino de los dioses
no quita que tengamos hambres,
y deseamos tantas cosas.

Ese que te abraza y te besa
es un regalo a
mi nueva reina,
diosa que pisa ahora en la tierra
haciendo mis trabajos.

Esto, me lo dijo Tatehuarí
no en un sueño
pero cuando estaba con ojos abiertos—
gozándote, gozándote.

—1997, *Chicago*

Tatehuarí*

Tatehuarí
came and told me:
Muchacha!
If I wasn't as old
as the hills,
the sierra,
or peyote,
I would make you mine
right this minute.

Muchacha!
This man, black
as chocolate and
sweet as a stewed
nopal, is my gift
to you
and will take my place.

Since clouds
have no flesh
and air
has no bones,
since I love you
the way I do,
and you are in the world.

*Tatehuarí: Ancient god of Huichol people of Mexico.

In the kingdom of the gods
it's still possible to go hungry.
We want so many things.

He who holds you and kisses you
is a gift to my
new queen,
the goddess that steps on the earth
doing my chores.

This is what Tatehuarí
said to me,
not in a dream,
but as I lay with my eyes
wide open,
enjoying you, enjoying you.

—Translated by Rosario Ferré

I Decide Not to Fall in Love

I almost fell in love with you
almost, my hand fell across
your clean indio chest,
that close to my ears and heart
were to your laughter when
you pulled on your boots,
slipped out
and I, wrapped in wool
without you, slept alone again,
I decided then not to,
not to, not to.

—1997, *Chicago*

Y ¿dónde se encuentra Dios?

La muerte es una mujer, Juana de Isbaje,
según el pensamiento que acompaña tu lenguaje.

También la vida es una mujer,
como la tierra es otra, amplia, y ancha.

En tus tiempos, la mar, terriblemente llena,
así mismo fue hembra.
La luna y su corte ilustra de doncellas, también
son grandes señoras.

Sólo el cielo pertenece al hombre.
De todo grande y pequeño, nomás el cielo
no es de Ella.

—1997, *Chicago*

Where Can We Find God?

Death is a woman, Juana de Isbaje,
in the thoughts that accompany your language.

Life is also a woman,
and earth is the other one, wide and generous.

In your time, the sea, staggeringly full,
was a woman, too.
The moon and its royal court of shining maidens
were all great ladies.

Only the sky belongs to man.
Among all things, big and small,
only the sky
did not belong to Her.

—Translated by Rosario Ferré

On the Meaning of Things

(In memory of Dieter Herms)

He took me to my first opera.
I was thirty-eight and he was dying.
He looked elegantly gaunt rather than infirm
in an off-white double-breasted jacket
suitable for summer.

It was *Don Giovanni*, in Italian with
German subtitles projected onto a screen.
"The plot is rather stupid," he said and already knew,
but enjoyed hearing Mozart again, the high point for him
being when he recognized an aria and could place it
into the story with his eyes closed.

He was intent throughout, near faint
with the thinness of air, the zithery music,
the crowded theater
and constant drilling pain.
At intermission, he reserved a table
and we had champagne.

"This will be the last time we see each other,"
he said. "What is hardest for me to give up is memory."
I moved my seat closer to his. "Perhaps, memory too
will be transformed," I speculated,
as is all we can do
with the meaning of greetings and partings, and love
that resists death.

—1991, *Albuquerque, New Mexico*

Hummingbird Heart

(MARCEL AT SIX)

Hummingbird heart
with hummingbird hands.
Such a tentative rush
toward petal and scent.
The smallest child
with the grandest of hearts
takes it all in.

—1990, *Albuquerque, New Mexico*

Nani Worries About Her Father's Happiness
   in the Afterlife

He knew nothing about death,
before he died.
(None of us did.)
Then he died,
and I was left to wonder where he went.

The Nahuas sent their loved ones,
accompanied by an esquincle,
to travel for four years,
before reaching Mictlan:
Region of the Dead,
also called Ximoayan,
Place of the Fleshless.
Mictlan: The House of Quetzal Plumes,
where there is no time.

Jesus descended into Hell
for three days,
freed his predecessor, Adam,
and returned to Earth.

Oh—such stories I have heard!
Men and their inventions.
I did not know what to think.

I looked about the room, held the hand
turning cold in mine.

His mouth open, having gasped
a last breath of life.
He was no longer in a sweat.

I wished I knew where he was—
floating above, near the ceiling,
perhaps, like those near-death cases
report?

Was he pleased with our Christian
praying over the corpse,
my many kisses on his forehead,
our reluctance to leave him alone?

A cold winter Chicago night:
Ash Wednesday, February 28.
The uselessness of doctrine in
those times. Ma and I decided
two things with that in mind:
This is hell.
This is not the whole story.

—1991, *Albuquerque, New Mexico*

Día de muertos

The dead like all the things we do:
They eat calabaza and pan de yema;
drink chocolate, Pepsi, and cerveza fría.
They act like we do, carry their dead babies
on bony backs, play violin off-key, dance a jig.
They take bubble baths, and stroll
through the zócalo with their dead sweethearts.
The dead like the perfumed scent of tuberoses,
the grandeur of gladiolus, the color and faithfulness
of cempasuchil and cresta de gallo flowers.
The dead like attention.
They are not saints; they do not answer petitions,
are not open to negotiation.
God does not hear the dead, who are only
dreaming—
like those of us who think ourselves alive.

—1991, *Albuquerque, New Mexico*

How Does It Feel to Be Cruel to a Woman?

How does it feel to be cruel to a woman?
To lift her up in front of her children,
to have them shout
she wants you out of the house!
Does it hurt to know this about yourself?
I'm wondering but not asking you.
You are not a friend anymore,
no one I respect.
Talk your way out of that one.
Tell everyone: *she* was psychotic.
Say: she doesn't care about her children
for letting you in in the first place,
for trying to love and be loved.
This is not a poem,
not for you.
It is a declaration
of allegiance to myself.

—1997, *Chicago*

For My Child Who Became a Man
in His Thirteenth Year

One night without ceremony
you became a man.
It happens all the time
in storybooks with
young warriors and knights
but not always in life.
Of you my son
I can testify.
You stood up,
wiry but determined.
You stood tall without notice
like something that had slept
a long time and suddenly had woken.
"I will love you no matter what," you pledged
as you set out to slay the dragon.
It was not Chinese or Chaucerian,
not even Mexican.
But it was very real.
It did not die but was wounded
and retreated.
Later, it tried to return, apologize.

"Fine," you said, "apologize all you like,
but you cannot come back."
Together you and I moved
from the kingdom of scaly,
slimy things that I used to not

so quickly recognize and
that you at thirteen, with courage
and imagination, banished
from our lives.

—1997, *Chicago*

A Little Prayer for the Trees

(For Chico Mendes)

I wonder if in heaven
Someone sees
how each day
an acre is felled
somewhere in the world.

We will all die
a more or less natural death.
But I pray that Someone Big
with Big words,
Big voice
above or on earth,
beyond or below,
will raise a Big hand
and stop
the killing of the trees.

—1997, *Chicago*

For Alberto and Selena

Not only the beautiful die young,
with her lover's name and a sigh
on raspberry-stained lips,
before her heart stopped beating.
But the rest of us, also, will die,
each and every one, all
with lesser or greater drama.

The life left unfinished,
a story without end,
will be picked up by those who knew us
and those who never did.
They will wear our shoes when no one is looking.
They will strut about in our wigs and underwear.
They will imagine themselves as if in a play,
with a plot about someone who may have shone
too brightly or not enough,
who may or may not have been loved.

No one is very certain about anything after a while.
They will surely say, "What a pity!"
whether we have died beautiful or had begun to rot.
At least, dear Alberto, I would like to think
it will be this way.

—2000, *Chicago*

Death Is Only What It Is

Death is not a man,
and certainly not a woman:
a crone on a horse cart
as some New Mexicans believed.

Death does not judge.
It is nothing but definite,
neat as a cotton handkerchief,
folded inside a breast pocket.

You only have a glimpse
and know it is there,
complete.

Even as I write these lines,
I know one day, too, I
will be dead.
You, who read them, also,
will have your turn.

It's best not to make
too much of it.
Death is only what it is,
no more and, indeed,
never less.

Peel My Love Like an Onion

Peel my love like an onion,
one transparent layer follows the next,
an infinity of desire.
I breathe your skin
and a vapor of memory arises,
tears my orifices raw
with the many smells of you.
When you leave, Tezcatlipoca,*
it is I who have evaporated you perhaps.
Horned creature to whom
I have given wings, come back. Rest again, in my
thin arms, limb with limb
like gnarled branches entwined in a sleep
of a thousand years.

*Pre-Conquest Mexican Night Sky God, primarily the god of providence.

Los Tocayos*

The man who grazed my flesh
wore your name—slanted
over the brow, like a pirate's hat
with a huge violet plume.
Such a grand and elegant name
with untold possibilities,
a name for men who wear gaucho boots,
and those who aim at women between the eyes for sport.

In time, you, too, will fit your name, no doubt,
slip it off with finesse
like the silk shirt left at the foot of my bed,
that you slipped on again,
with the same silent ease
before light, when I—as I did with him—
sent you away.

—1991, *Albuquerque, New Mexico*

*Two persons with the same name; connotes that they have a special kinship
as a result.

For Elsa

Cleopatra—
a woman I admired more
when I thought
she was black—
(having had my fill of Greeks and Romans)
took the pearl her suitor
offered
and dropped it in
a chalice
to melt in wine
thus prove how unimpressed
she was
with his gift and his size—
that is, leader of the biggest, baddest
nation at the time
or trying to be.

It's the kind of thing queens do,
place the stakes real high
for their love.
Pearls not being grand enough
or rather, meant for the common woman,
one day he killed himself for her
and she for him.
Their children also died.

Such was the price
and always will be
for forbidden love
even for a queen.

—1997, Chicago

I Am Not Egyptian

I

"I am not Egyptian," you wrote
when the woman you have loved
against your own wishes since time began
has spelled your name wrong again.

She is calling you, misspelled woman,
Egyptian or not,
from the great expanse of her bed
like Noah's Ark,
during a tropical storm.

I am calling you.
I am only one
and only two will do.

II

Why are you so jealous with me?
You—whose father is the sun
and your wife the most luminous star of all.
The galaxy and earth and all things grand and small
are yours. What could I give you
but a night that no one sees?
So what if I forget your name,
beautiful and distant as Isis.
It is you whom I want.
Don't fret so,
if I don't love you,
I don't love anyone else either.

—1997, *Cuernavaca, México*

All I Have for Her Is a Poem

María Magdalen sends me lace, perfumed soaps,
chocolates on Wednesdays and long-stemmed roses
for no occasion, Mexican gold and Italian filigree—
a diamond ring from her finger.
As if I were a lady of leisure, she ships
paints and brushes so that I may idle away
my Sundays. María Magdalen gives herself no pleasure
but the one of giving to me.
Her gifts come wrapped in flowered tissue,
with handwritten notes, letters lavender scented.
The postmaster wonders who are all the admirers.
It is Magdalen alone, I tell him,
an angel banished from heaven,
fallen to earth
as a woman.

—1991, *Albuquerque, New Mexico*

María's Clock Is Alive

María's clock is alive.
So I offer it some apple slices,
which it spits out. I pretend not to be afraid.
I whisper to María (trying on a tight,
brown wool skirt I have just given her)
that I *like* her clock.
I am ready for it when it comes looking for me.
I have gathered my own reserve of menacing clocks
around me. We howl and wail.
Soon, María in the tight skirt comes running
to see what all the commotion is about.

—1989, *Chico, California*

Seduced by Nastassia Kinski

I always had a thing for Nastassia Kinski—
My Sorbonne clique and I went to see her latest film.
Giant billboards all over Paris: Nastassia—
legs spread, her lover's face lost in between.

I watched *Paris, Texas,* twice, in Paris
remembering those lips in *Tess,* biting
into a fleshy strawberry.

So, long after I have gotten over Nastassia Kinski, I
am with a new Chicago clique, on holiday.
I have become an atom
in ungraspable flux,
ever-changing, multiplying—
when my Bavarian babushka is pulled off
from around my neck. It is Nastassia.

She has removed her KGB black leather coat; bottom of
the ocean eyes are working me and, yes, that mouth . . .
So when we dance, I avoid her gaze, I am trying
every possible way to escape eyes, mouth, smile,
    determination,
scarf pulling me closer, cheap wine, strobe light, dinner
    invitation:
come home with me. It's all for fun, she says.

I think: *I'll leave with someone else.*
But she finds me at a table in the dark. What

do you want—my money? I ask. She reminds me (cockily),
that she has more money than I do.
And when we dance again I am a strawberry, ripened
and bursting, devoured, and she has won.

We assure each other the next day, neither of us
has ever done anything like that before.

By Sunday night, we don't go out for dinner as planned.
Instead, over a bottle of champagne, Nastassia declares—
she wants me forever. Unable to bear that pouting mouth,
too sad for words, I whisper: *te llevaré conmigo*—
As if I had a choice.

—1989, *Santa Barbara, California*

One Thousand Nights

Once, I ran
inside a fairy book
to a princess,
who was an Arabian colt,
shiny mane and vacant eyed.
We lived amidst plastic flamingos, a thick
clutter of basic pumps, French perfume, and barbells.
She slept in zebra print spandex pants
bought on Venice Beach,
on a mattress with no sheets.
When she menstruated, she wore the same panties
all week.
She kept eight pillows: six beneath her head,
one to hug throughout the night, and the last,
stuck between her thighs.
Her thoroughbred's diet consisted of: tuna, spaghetti with no
    sauce,
cases of diet Coke, and plenty of hay.

She was spoiled beyond repair. In a bad mood
she spit between her teeth.
I was too quick for her aim.
She scrawled threats in red lipstick
on the bathroom mirror, pried into my diary,
and tore the pages out of my address book.

Every morning I made *her* cappuccino and
tried to book a flight out—

trapped and destined to a horrid fate of fiction—
I was sure.

As it happened—
we parted one day by accident. I was on my way
to catch the train to see a film about a gestapo agent when
—1989, *Santa Barbara, California*

When Women Part

There is no diamond ring to pawn,
no wedding band to flush down the drain,
nor family heirlooms to return:
when women part—
it is a simple affair.
No court threats for child custody:
One is the mother,
the other is not.
Wise friends maintain diplomacy, relatives:
their usual discretion.
They divide belongings in a practical manner,
couch, bed, shared underwear.
Books, music, pictures—are other matters.
Finally it is all done.
A life together: an aberration.

When women part rage is a stone
buried four thousand years ago,
and no one recalls where.

—1989, *Santa Barbara, California*

For a Toltec Queen

A man is not a god,
don't you know?
He is not your father
although he may protect you
from the things of his own making.

A woman is not a god either,
made only of flesh and bones,
the same substance as you.
Augustine thought her disgusting,
as did most martyrs and saints.

Repulsive for our abundance,
a grandness of fortitude—I say!
Spoiled princess of doting lovers and fathers—
come away with me, come away.

—1997, *Chicago*

She Was Brave to Leave You

She was brave to leave you,
to buy a ticket in secret,
kiss you as if it were just
another afternoon,
and catch the first plane out
far away.
She was brave,
she whispered to herself and giggled,
wiped her brow hot with sweat,
as she waited for the plane to take off.

She only wished that every woman
who sat by a window,
who stood by the door
watching the soup simmer,
put salve on the purple bruises on her arms,
or kept hidden the nasty things said to her
that morning,
tucked away in a journal,
as hidden as the yearning in her heart
was just as brave.
She imagined him later
running at night
wild with rage and drunk,
through the bare fields of winter vines,
the olive groves,
among the fig trees,

naked, his buttocks scratched,
knees and forearms from thorns
and the jagged pricks of dried branches.

She imagined he wouldn't call out her name
not so much as a whisper
the moon a crescent-shaped sickle
glistening in the sky brimming with Roman stars.
She imagined how his laughter bellowed through
the air because another undeserving woman had left him.

In her own first night, far away, she dreamed of a fish with
    bones.
Its eyes bulged out at her from the plate,
its penis still alive.
She brought the not-so-dead thing to her mouth and ate.
She sucked on a dozen pomegranates with a multitude of
    seeds,
then woke with blood and an empty womb.
She asked a friend: "Do you think I've gone mad?"
The friend replied with a solemn no.
Still, she wondered what had happened to her ears,
her eyes, her sense of smell. Everything was silent.
Her friend took her hand. "You're cold."
"Yes, I am always cold," she said.
"I'll put another log in the fire," her friend offered.
"No, don't," she said. "Don't."

—1999, *Chicago*

While I Was Gone a War Began

While I was gone a war began.
Every day I asked friends in Rome
to translate the news.
It seems I saw this story
in a Hollywood movie,
or on a Taco Bell commercial,
maybe in an ad for sunglasses
or summer wear—shown somewhere
for promotional purposes.

Hadn't I seen it in an underground cartoon,
a sinister sheikh versus John Wayne?
Remembering Revelation I wanted to laugh,
the way a nonbeliever remembers Sunday School
and laughs, which is to say—
after flood and rains,
drought and despair,
abrupt invasions,
disease and famine everywhere,
we're still left dumbfounded
at the persistence of fiction.

While I was gone
continents exploded—
the Congo, Ireland,
Mexico, to name a few places.
At this rate, one day soon

they won't exist at all.
It's only a speculation, of course.

"What good have all the great writers done?"
an Italian dissident asked, as if
this new war were my personal charge.
"What good your poems,
your good intentions,
your thoughts and words
all for the common good?
What lives have they saved?
What mouths do they feed?
What good is your blue passport
when your American plane blows up?"
the Italian dissident asked in a rage.
"Forced out of his country,
the poor African selling trinkets in Italy,
does not hesitate to kill other blacks
not of his tribe.
Who is the bad guy? Who is the last racist?
Who colonizes in the twenty-first century best:
the Mexican official over the Indian
or the gringo ranchero over the Mexican illegal?
"I hope for your sake your poems become missiles,"
the dissident said. He lit a cigarette, held it to his yellowed
    teeth.
"I hope for my sake, too. I tried," he said.
"I did not write books or have sons
but I gave my life
and now, I don't care."

Again, I had nothing to give but a few words
which I thought then to keep to myself
for all their apparent uselessness.
We drank some wine, instead,
made from his dead father's vineyard.
We trapped a rat getting into the vat.
We watched another red sun set over the fields.
At dawn, I left,
returned to the silence of the press
when it has no sordid scandal to report.
As if we should not be scandalized
by surprise bombing over any city at night,
bombs scandalizing the sanctity of night.

—1998, *Chicago*

A Federico García Lorca más a algunos otros

I once went to a costume ball
as García Lorca
After the Assassination—
suitably bullet ridden
blood drenched: a macabre
and ironic vision
of poetic justice.

I prepared for weeks.
Along the streets of San Francisco
I went about the business
of the poet.
I met and laughed with poet friends
in our favorite cafes.
We edited a paper.
We talked about the war.
We were befittingly outraged.
As I said, I went about the business
of the poet.

The time came to hide.

I searched frantically for safety
among family.
I was afraid of death.
But the world has no lack of
traitors and infidels.

I was lined up with a schoolteacher,
a few others known to think
about things.
I alone was shot in the ass
for being a queer—
Pas! Pas! Pas!
Zas! Zas! Zas!
My ghost danced on Franco's head
in the body of a woman with a false mustache,
fifty years to the day—
triumphant and glorious
breasts bouncing to a samba rhythm.

Poeta que no dejaste de amar: je t'aime.
And I will dance for you
until they come and drag me away:
bragging illiterate fools,
who did not even know your name
will remember mine
and Lucha's
Francisco's
Juan Pablo's
Rodrigo's
Barbara's, Ester's, Juana Alicia's, Yolanda's,
and all the Marías,
Ricardo from El Salvador
in red shirt and suspenders,
Miguel recruiting disciples for Oaxaca,
Piri mellowed after *Mean Streets,*
Gato's, Linda's, Marcel—

the "Little Prince": *my* child was there;
La India Bonita Cross-dresser Bar taking a collection
for the funerals of every other Monday.
And they will try
to be rid of us
any way *they* can.
Call *them* by name these "they."
Point fingers in turn—*You:*
who sent us to Panama and Saudi Arabia—
with a bribe of college tuition, a mortgage loan,
and bad medical care,
so merciless and trigger-happy—*try*
to be rid of us.

We rise out of the ground
like margaritas,
yerba buena,
blades of grass, we the poets,
painters, a merry band of dissonant musicians.
Too many of us and too much for you
to silence with the yanking of one pure
voice
that rose
from the ashes of butterflies and doves
to call you   by name.

                                —1990, *Albuquerque, New Mexico*

For James Baldwin, with Love (November 8, 1989)

> I've loved a few men and a few women. . . .
> In strange packages . . . the trick is to say yes to life.
> — JAMES BALDWIN*

You chose, as I choose
to despair, or not
on a given night or day.
That despair turned inside out
you called love.

What is it like now, in a place
where there are no illusions
of democracy?

—1989, *Santa Barbara, California*

*From the film *James Baldwin in Another Place*.

Poeta en Santa Fe

(a Federico García Lorca)

La silla. Chair.
La mesa al lado de la silla. Table next to the chair.
Pan duro y vino sobre la mesa. Hard bread and wine on the
    table.
Sol frío como en tu país sobre tus hombros desnudos
Cold sun as it is in your country against bare shoulders
En el atardecer. At sunset.

Aire mordaz de diciembre   Bitter air of December
pica tu rostro.   nips at your face.
Todo es silencio.   Everything is silent.

Él no está.   He is gone.

                 —1990, *Albuquerque, New Mexico*

Chi-Town Born and Bred, Twentieth-Century Girl
Propelled with Flare into the Third Millennium

(For Nelson and Simone)

I'll turn into an 8
if I am late! Said the Mad Hatter
of Chicago, City on the Make
that got put through Rehab, a Twelve Step Program or two,
sent the Mayor's brother to Washington to give the party a
    hand,
gutted out warehouses, tore up factories,
and leveled down docks.

It's a truly *beau-ti-ful* town now.

Clean as polished chrome if not always sober.
Although debauchery is not tolerated, not even at Wrigley
    Field
when the Cubs lose again despite Sammy Sosa,
or at the United Center after a Blackhawks game, not even
    when
the Bulls won their sixth championship.
Not an odoriferous trace of the fish market or
of the stockyards that once were our trademark.

The river beats the Seine for clarity, and the lake
is not just a lake but a Mediterranean Lite.
The Buckingham Fountain still infuses June nights at Grant
    Park
for free music lovers and lovers of every other kind.
Yes. It's a pretty city if you're not down on your luck

or being relocated from Cabrini Green
to something else like it or you're not locked up in County Jail
or sleeping on cardboard in the Jewel's parking lot.
No clotheslines-on-porches views from the El train
anymore but flower boxes and portable barbecues.
Every window from North to South and even on State Street
right downtown is to a condo, a computer hack's office,
an architect's studio ringside seat of the winning skyline to
    heaven
that all of Asia cannot beat.

Don't get me wrong.
The American Dream stories that this city was known for
one hundred years ago more than still abound
right here in Uptown. Across the street Africans pray
on Sunday morning for asylum, Salvadoran refugees and
    Mexican
illegals lie low waiting for appointments with the Immigration
    Service.
D.P.s are darker now; seem less hopeful than the Europeans I
    knew
growing up near Maxwell Street:
Italian markets with dry hanging bacalao and live snails in
    baskets,
Jews in doorways with their fine tailoring and pawnshops,
the Irish cops and mafia bosses and Greek restaurants
along Halsted Street, gypsy fortune tellers and no-name dere-
    licts
loitering near Madison—everything so unapologetically eth-
    nically

and economically divided. All this I saw, growing up as Mary
    Ann,
little Mexican girl who went to Jane Addams' charitable man-
    sion
to learn to cook and stitch and to stay off the streets.

My mother named me Ana María, which got purposely
    turned around
at the hospital like everything an Indian woman said and did
    got turned around.
In public school I was renamed Marie like a missionary's
    convert
and later back to Mary Ann, but at home I was Anita.
To my father: Anna Magnani—the movie star.
He was born in Chicago too. I went to the same grammar
    school
he had but not the same high school because by then it was
    1968:
The Democratic Convention, Martin Luther King came
    around
and racial intolerance was going every which way
with brown people kept in between.
If you're white, you're all right.
If you're brown stick around.
If you're black—step back, step back, step back, step back. But
if you were brown in the white part of town or wandered to
    the South Side,
which was black back then, you had better run and run fast.
The man I called my father was a tough young lad on the
    fence

between a punk and respectable head of the family.
After a while he straightened up.
He did not believe in upward mobility or even lateral mobility.
He liked things to stay the same. The city came and moved us
when it was time to bulldoze our neighborhood near little Italy
to build a university.
He worked on and off in factories and smoked a lot of
    cigarettes.
The last company closed down and packed off to Southeast
    Asia.
He died, one winter night, unemployed.

His mother got to Chicago chasing a son
who took off with Pancho Villa, but all that—
as they say—is history.
She was Pentecostal and a curandera,
penniless as they get.
I wish she'd been a bootlegger.
I wish she'd have married a crooked police chief
and left me a lot of money hidden in an old trunk.
Instead, she left me the legacy of being Mexican
this far north where being Mexican was not just beans and
    tortillas
all day, all night, Mary Ann,
and not just English lilts but a tilted Spanish too.
That eradicable accent which came from being the child of
    factory workers,
field workers, railroad workers, and related to every kind of
    labor work
in the Midwest is all your people ever knew.

One day after my son was born I took my name back and left.
We lived all over the country.
We saw the big cities and stayed in a lot of small towns.
We went to corn dances at Laguna Pueblo
and learned to eat lobster in Gloucester.
We sat by the seashore in California and got the grand tour of
   Texas.
We came back unimpressed and stayed.
Now my son is a bona-fide Chicagoan. He's a product
of his generation or maybe mine, the free-lovin'
seventies, when reading and travels opened our imagination,
which is to say he's proud to be a mutt-boy like all his friends.
If they're not they invent a combination.
They're not brown or black or white or even Cantonese
like the food in Chinatown but a true molcajete grind.
They don't hustle on the street. They don't have the blues.
They paint their names on notebooks and don't violate public
   property.
They rhyme words and scratch old LPs and call it music.
Late into the night they talk about the revolution but
as far as I can tell not one last one can say a revolution of
   what.
They're pros at video games but none would carry a real gun.
So all this is to say that just maybe my hometown won't
have been totally shot to hell by the year 2001.

No more penny candy stores,
no more taverns on the corner with pee- and beer-stained
   floors,
and fathers whose children have to come in and drag on home.

Not many hot dog/beef stands left but commerce is booming
     on a grand scale
with a vague imitation of all that once was.
New bars, shops, cinema multiplexes, the same you'd find
anywhere. Forget about it! From Canada to Mexico!
What with the Free Trade Agreement in full swing
it's soon to be one big theme park. One day it'll look like
     Orlando.
All that'd be missing are the palm-tree-lined boulevards.
Ethnics have taken over the burbs.
Asians and Arabs have taken off with the franchises.
The Children of the White Flight have come back to roost.
Raised on liberals' pablum they like to think they have no
     prejudices. Heck, they don't
scorn foreigners or bilingualism. They speak better Spanish
than their Nicaraguan nannies. It is an age of investments
     and portfolios
but they don't like the word *capitalist,* which rings of Republi-
     can and hard
on the ears of a democratic town.
(But if Colin Powell ever decides to run for President no one
     will ever
be sure again which party is which.)
Nostalgia's the trend. Frank Sinatra's "Chicago"
plays on jukeboxes like a Disney movie score from yesteryear.
How can any of these newcomers—with their jeeps
and scuba-diving equipment and books recommended on-line
and coffee from Kenya and microbeer savoir-faire,
who think they could hold a conversation with Hemingway
because they've gone on kangaroo hunts in Australia

organized by Safaris Are Us and are bronze all year around
     from
tanning booths and play golf on weekends with the boss—
lay claim to this town?

But they don't. The truth is they don't even want it.
They don't want anything for very long.
Today you try what suits you and when it don't—
move on, move on, move on.
I'll turn into an 8 if I am late.
I traded in my hat for a hundred pairs of imported shoes.
They're not for beating the pavement but for show.
The world is my oyster too, you know,
said the mad cobbler out loud. If you don't think that way,
if you don't shake a leg and become a pack of one,
this city like any other, don't matter if it's San Francisco
gone Silicon or overcrowded Manhattan,
it doesn't matter if it's French-Creole New Orleans
turned capital of Honduras,
doesn't matter how much times have changed,
looking so much easier in some ways but just as
tricky to get over than ever, Chicago will eat you up just like that.
Spit you out a fate worse than death:
Keep you anonymous no matter what you try.
You can get on a talk show and say trash about your grandma
or take a job as a cook and call yourself a chef tomorrow
or start your own digital-movie industry right at home.
Big Brother is not a threat but now a TV program watching you
pick your teeth on video.
You can do whatever you want.

when fame is the only game in town.
But Chicago—like Madrid or Rome or L.A.,
like Maui or Maine—
you've got to treat right.
Don't hold back your best. Keep vanity in check.
Watch whose toes you step on on the way up.
Chicago will not forget and it will show you the way down
on the rush hour elevator express.
Next winter the wind chill will be steadily colder than the
    year before.
You'll find yourself changing residences to some nearby town
or where you have to catch a plane or boat to get there,
pretending you've left because it's better somewhere else.
But like any loser knows you'll know:
There's no place like Sweet Home Chicago
when you're on top of the world.

Canto para las brujas of Good Deeds and Desires

¡Saludos hermanas mías!

We salute our mothers,
our mothers' mothers
and our fathers' mothers.
They are the women who helped
guide our souls to this path.

We salute our fathers
and their ancestors
who also have guided our path.

We salute all those who share
our table with us.

We salute those who work
with us.
We are working women,
daughters of mothers who also worked
to bring food to their families' tables.
We honor all work
that enables us to nurture ourselves,
our families, those with whom we share
our lives, our table.

We salute our friends and relations.
We wish them health and good dreams
to sustain them.

We wish the success of their dreams,
that all their deeds be good
and bring their lives enrichment.

We pray for the health of those we love
who have fallen ill.
We wish them spiritual strength
and the light that will guide them
peacefully to health or transition
if that be their souls' choice.

We pray that our government's leaders
look into their souls,
that they think with the heart of a mother
in making the decisions that affect
the world's populations.

We pray for the artists, field workers,
and the homeless. May they find
food, decent shelter, and beauty in their lives
to sustain them.

We pray for the souls of those we brought
into this world and those we chose not to.

We pray for each other
and for the strength to overcome
all challenges.

We pray that our deepest desires be fulfilled,
to the extent that they are wise and good
for our lives, our souls, and those we love.
We pray for the wisdom always to know how
to serve not only our own people but all people,
for service is the way of the Xicana.
We pray for joy and love to fill our hearts,
our days and our nights,
for joy and love is also the way
of Xicanisma, a noble way,
a way of honor and dignity.

It is the way of the Nahua,
Aztec, Maya, Huichol, Tarahumara,
Purépucha, Otomí, Zapotec—all our ancestors,
all women and men who came before us
and are here with us.
It is the way of the Toltec.
We honor them through our acts, and by pursuing our desires
and dreams
that are the dreams and desires
of our divinities
and therefore ours.

Buenas noches y hasta la próxima,
hermanas mías.

—1996, Chicago